Divine Love ♥ Twin Flames

With quotes from A Course in Miracles

Paula Rule

All quotes from A Course in Miracles are from
the Combined Volume Third Edition 2007
© Foundation for Inner Peace
P.O. Box 598
Mill Valley, CA 94942-0598
www.acim.org and
info@acim.org

Material from A Course in Miracles is used with
permission from the publisher, copyright holder,
The Foundation for Inner Peace.

Cover Image:
Two of Cups from the Star Tarot by Cathy McClelland

Image Credit: Bigstock

ISBN: 978-0-6489221-0-0 Paperback
      978-0-6489221-1-7 eBook

© Paula Rule 2020

https://www.goldenraytwinflameearthangel.com

All Rights Reserved

Contents

Welcome	1
What is a Miracle?	9
Christ Consciousness	19
Divine Love 💗 Twin Flames	27
He is My Twin	51
My Twin Soul	53
Universal Self	57
Heart Chakra – Universal CPU	65
Purity and Sacred Sexuality	71
Transcendental Chakras	75
The 'Clairs'	81
New Earth Community	85
Rainbow Rays	91
The Last Judgement	95
Links	97
About the author	99

Divine Love ♥ Twin Flames

With quotes from A Course in Miracles

Welcome

Divine love leads to revelation and expression of universal self. When we communicate with the heart, we enter quantum time. The matrix dissolves to reveal the eternal light beings we are. Twin Flames arise to their sacred purpose as archetypes of divine love for the foundation of new earth community.

We are made to be miracle workers on the golden path of Christ Consciousness. Awakening to this truth includes your unique purpose in the new paradigm. What transcendental abilities are dormant within you, waiting to be discovered and expanded? This is an exciting beginning for everyone who hears the call of awakening and ascension.

All of us have a divine mission in the creation of new earth community. 'golden ray twin flame earth angel' - is just my job description as a light worker. Christ Consciousness is the desire of a golden ray and divine love is my passion. Energetic healers of all rays are empowered to restore our soul tribes and our home. We are powerful creators and manifesters, upgraded to return our earth to paradise.

Inspired writings can help to release ego perception for good. I often read inspirational books where the authors credited A Course in Miracles. I bought my own copy in divine timing, at the beginning of my Twin Flame journey. I was amazed to learn the text was divinely inspired, automatic writing by a clinical psychologist. A woman indoctrinated in the system, focusing on

Welcome

the mental body. This is a miracle in itself as the messages are truly spiritual.

The content of this book was so deep I often passed out or had to nap from the intensity. One verse can literally open your heart to a whole new level, and many light the Twin Flame path and the way to new earth community.

A Course in Miracles may seem daunting due to its length – and depth, but prophetic truth dissolves mental blocks, opens the heart chakra and awakens dormant DNA for divine connection.

All your past except its beauty is gone; and nothing is left but a blessing. I have saved all your kindnesses and every loving thought you ever had. I have purified them of the errors that hid their light, and kept them for you in their own perfect radiance. T-5.IV.8:2-4

The above quote from A Course in Miracles can reflect you and your life but how do you get to that place? How do you let go of everything you think you are? What does it mean to surrender?

Hear, then, the one answer of the Holy Spirit to all the questions the ego raises: You are a child of God, a priceless part of His kingdom, which He created as part of Him. T-6.IV:1

A deep peace and joy is known to those devoted to their soul path. These earthangels demonstrate high frequency love and show the way to growth no matter how difficult the journey may seem. They communicate from the heart chakra and complete what they came to this world to do.

The great peace of the Kingdom shines in your mind forever, but it must shine outward to be aware of it. Each of us is the light of the world, and by joining our minds in this light we proclaim the Kingdom of God together and as one. T-6.12:8

Welcome

When we truly love ourselves and each other we create communities of light, where the only law is universal law and the only rule is the golden rule.

The ego is Legion, but the Holy Spirit is One. The ego is afraid of the spirit's joy, because once you have experienced it you will withdraw all protection from the ego, and become totally without investment in fear. Listen only to God.
T-6.II.13:2-5

What is a Miracle?

What is a Miracle?

A miracle is a service. It is the maximal service you can render to another. It is a way of loving your neighbour as yourself. You recognise your own and your neighbour's worth simultaneously. T-1.I.18:2-4

Miracles make minds one in God. They depend on cooperation because the Sonship is the sum of all that God created. Miracles therefore reflect the laws of eternity, not of time. T-1.I.19.:1-3

God has given you a place in His mind that is yours forever. Yet you can only keep it by giving it, as it was given you. To give without limit is God's will for you, because only this can bring you the joy that is His and that He wills to share with you. Your love is as boundless as His because it is His. T-11.I.6:1-2, 7-8

The more love you give the more blessed you feel. You will know the wonder of miracles through the power of universal love. Caring for yourself increases your ability to care for others. You may feel damaged by the past but you can be completely healed and heal others as well.

Health is inner peace. It enables you to remain unshaken by lack of love from without and capable, through your acceptance of miracles, of correcting the conditions proceeding from lack of love in others. T-2.I.5:11-12

You don't have to go looking for miracles as the soul path is lit with them. Let go the uncertainty of the ego matrix and embrace the truth of your soul. Nurture peace in your spirit and develop

What is a Miracle?

your power to manifest miracles. Divine child, the dignity of a beautiful spirit is yours forever.

You can do anything I ask. I have asked you to perform miracles, and have made it clear that miracles are natural, corrective, healing and universal. The children of God are entitled to the perfect comfort that comes from perfect trust. They must learn to look upon the world as a means of healing the separation. The atonement is the guarantee that they will ultimately succeed. T-2.II:1-2, T-2.III.5:1, 12-13

Those who witness for me are expressing, through their miracles, that they have abandoned the belief in deprivation in favour of the abundance they have learned belongs to them. T-1.IV.4:8

Miracles occur in the eternal Now moment where the past, present and future come together with your sacred desire to serve.

The Holy instant is the result of your determination to be holy. It is the answer. The desire and the willingness to let it come precede its coming. You prepare your mind for it by recognising that you want it above all else. The Holy Spirit joins with you to make the holy instant far greater than you can understand. The miracle of the Holy instant lies in your willingness to let it be what it is. And in your willingness for this lies your acceptance of yourself as you were meant to be. T-18.IV:1-4, 8-9.

You can also harmonize with universal love through prayer; and when your life is your prayer you create miracles, open hearts and touch souls intimately with your thoughts, words and deeds.

I offer you only the recognition of His power in you, but in that lies all truth. The miracles we do bear witness to the Will of the Father for His son and to our joy in uniting with His Will for us. T-8.V.3:3, 7.

What is a Miracle?

Anyone can participate in the creation of miracles. Now is the time to transcend the ego matrix as Twin Flames of all Rays help our brothers and sisters to arise and thrive in the energy of the spirit.

I can inspire a mind
touch a heart
ignite a soul
through the power of Love
I Am a Child of God.

Paula Rule 2014

Christ Consciousness

Christ Consciousness

Oh my child, if you knew what God wills for you, your joy would be complete! And what He wills has happened, for it was always true. When the light comes and you have said, 'Gods will is mine,' you will see such beauty that you will know it is not of you. T-11.III.3:1-3

Out of your joy you will create beauty in His name, for your joy could no more be contained than His. The bleak little world will vanish into nothingness, and your heart will be so filled with joy that it will leap into Heaven, and into the Presence of God. T-11.III.3:4-5

Who was He?

He was born into the injustice and suffering of the ego matrix with awareness of His soul purpose. His heavenly Father instructed Him to teach us the truth of our power but only those who were pure of heart could begin to understand and try to follow Him.

He was made to grow through experience. He felt hunger, cold, exhaustion and pain through devotion to His path. Caring for His brothers and sisters in spirit amplified His knowledge of love, sorrow, joy and grief. He taught spiritual truth and worked miracles of healing, advocating for those suffering injustice.

He did not cater to the ego trips of others and spoke out against the hypocrisy of ruling religious leaders, saying, "You snakes! You brood of vipers! How will you escape being condemned to hell? Matthew 23:33

Christ Consciousness

He lost patience with the disciples who were still slaves to cultural conditioning, doubt and fear; exclaiming, "O faithless generation, how long shall I be with you? How long shall I suffer you?" Mark 9:19

He was hit with hatred and rejection from the powerful in the ego matrix... as are we who follow Him.

He knew He would soon be murdered and left them with instruction for awakening and ascension. A new command I give you: Love one another. As I have loved you, so you must love one another. John 13:34

In this world you can become a spotless mirror, in which the Holiness of your Creator shines forth from you to all around you. T-14.IX.5:1

We are mirrors for each other. Some reflect back love and others don't want to see how negative their energy is. They may break the mirror but they can't erase the reflection of beauty and fulfilment they glimpsed in themselves.

Only Gods comforter can comfort you. In the quiet of His temple, He waits to give you the peace that is yours. Give His peace, that you may enter the temple and find it waiting for you. T-11.III.7:1-3

The Holy Spirit, whom the Father will send in my name, he will teach you all things and bring to your remembrance all that I have said to you. John 14:26

The call to Christ Consciousness is a call to action, to live and share divine love. Twin Flames arise as a phoenix of light for the dawning of new earth community.

Christ Consciousness

The power of God, from which they both arise, is yours as surely as it is His. You think you know Him not only because, alone, it is impossible to know Him. Yet see the mighty works that He will do through you, and you must be convinced you did them through Him. It is impossible to deny the Source of effects so powerful they could not be of you. Leave room for Him, and you will find yourself so filled with power that nothing will prevail against your peace. And this will be the test by which you recognise that you have understood.

T-14.XI.15:1-6

Your will be done, you holy child of God. What your Father wills for you can never change. The truth in you remains as radiant as a star, as pure as light, as innocent as love itself. And you are worthy that your will be done. T-31.VI.7:1-5

Divine Love ♥ Twin Flames

Divine Love 💗 Twin Flames

In each the other saw a perfect shelter where his Self could be reborn in safety and in peace.
T-22.I.9:8

A Twin is your cosmic mirror. The connection is profound and undeniable. It is the highest energy for remembering and becoming your universal self.

The Holy Spirit within you has seen your brother, and recognised him perfectly since time began. And it desired nothing but to join with him and to be free again, as once it was.
T-21.IV.5:1-2

The ego self is overcome and released as universal love electrifies your chakras for ultimate awakening and ascension.

This sacred Son of God is like yourself; the mirror of his Father's love by which he was created and which still abides in him as it abides in you. T-29.V.4:1

Twin Flames are identical universal souls who recognize their sacred connection of innocence, purity and abundance.

Revelation induces complete but temporary suspension of doubt and fear. Revelation unites you directly with God. Miracles unite you directly with your brother. T-1.II:6-7

This revelation is accompanied by divine signs and symbols that elevate consciousness to celestial realms. During the 2012 Twin Flame awakening one of my sacred signs was a bird flying onto my balcony and ringing golden chimes hanging there.

The connection between Twins is beyond 3D logic, time and space. It has to be to overcome the ego self and live from the heart chakra that holds higher intelligence than the mainstream construct.

We go beyond the veil of fear, lighting each other's way. The holiness that leads us is within us, as is our home. The lamp is lit in you for your brother. And by the hand that gave it to him shall you be led past fear to love. T-20.II.9:4-5 T-20.II.11:6-7

Did you meet your brother with joy to bless the Son of God, and give him thanks for all the happiness that he held out to you? Did you recognize your brother as the eternal gift of God to you? Did you see the holiness that shone in both you and your brother, to bless the other? T-20.III.8:6-9

Much inner work is needed to rise up to the Twin Flame path and it can be a lonely and difficult path others just can't comprehend. Sometimes the pain of letting go of the past can be so intense it feels like dying; and it's in that moment your Twin's angelic self holds you close until you're strong enough to continue the sacred journey to reunion.

Be very still and hear Gods Voice in him, and let It tell you what his function is. He was created that you might be whole, for only the complete can be a part of God's completion, which created you. T-29.V.4:2-3

That is the purpose of your holy relationship. Here is only holiness and joining without limit. For what is Heaven but union, direct and perfect, and without the veil of fear upon it? Here we are one, looking with perfect gentleness upon each other and on ourselves.

T-20.III.8:9 T-20.III.10:3-4

Divine Love 💗 Twin Flames

Twin Flame union comes through healing yourself and your Twin. You will face and overcome your deepest fear to be reborn into the beauty and peace of universal love.

To heal, then, is to correct perception in your brother and yourself by sharing the Holy Spirit with him. This places you both within the Kingdom, and restores its wholeness in your mind. This reflects creation, because it unifies by increasing and integrates by extending.

T-7.II.2:1-3

There is a place in you which time has left, and echoes of eternity are heard. The changelessness of Heaven is in you, so deep within that nothing in this world but passes by, unnoticed and unseen. The still infinity of endless peace surrounds you gently in its soft embrace, so strong and quiet, tranquil in the might of its Creator, nothing can intrude upon the Sacred Son of God within. Accept the changeless and eternal that abide in him, for your Identity is there. The peace in you can but be found in him. And every thought of love you offer him but brings you nearer to your wakening to peace eternal and to endless joy.

T-29.V.1:2, 2:3-4, 3:4-5

The divine in me wanted to share my feelings with him but my ego self refused. I would rather die than inflate the ego of someone who already thought himself above others.

Know first that this is fear. Fear arises from lack of love. The only remedy for lack of love is perfect love. Perfect love is the Atonement.

T-2.VI.7:5-8

My stubborn refusal went on for two years until I was horribly injured and nearly died. It was then I understood I had to release all resistance and surrender to the prompting of the Holy Spirit.

Futility of function not fulfilled will haunt you while your brother lies asleep, till what has been assigned to you is done and he is risen from the past. T-24.VI.9:3

My Twin is someone my ego self would never consider. Yet the first time our eyes met, galaxies collided to reveal the Unified Field.

You who are dedicated to the incorruptible have been given through your acceptance, the power to release from corruption. The infancy of salvation is carefully guarded by love, preserved from every thought that would attack it, and quietly made ready to fulfil the mighty task for which it was given you. Your newborn purpose is nursed by angels, cherished by the Holy Spirit and protected by God himself. T-19.IV.C.6:1, I.9:3-4

In any situation in which you are uncertain, the first thing to consider, very simply, is 'What do I want to come of this? What is it for? The clarification of the goal belongs at the beginning. T-17.VI.2:1-3

The value of deciding in advance what you want to happen is simply that you will perceive the situation as a means to make it happen. You will therefore make every effort to overlook what interferes with the accomplishment of your objective, and concentrate on everything that helps you meet it. The goal of truth has further practical advantages. If the situation is used for truth and sanity, its outcome must be peace. T-17.VI.4:1-2,5:1

I revealed the truth of my heart in a poem to awaken my Twin. It was a complete letting go of fear and allowing the essence of my soul to bloom into the most beautiful expression of love. This was epic as I would have to release all resistance to someone fully invested in the world of the ego.

Truth comes of itself. If you experience peace, it is because the truth has come to you and you will see the outcome truly, for deception cannot prevail against you. T-17.VI.5:5-6

Shared beauty of spirit is realized every time I look in a mirror and see his eyes. How can someone I don't know touch and awaken my soul more than anyone, ever?

In the ego matrix, his attitude of pride and privilege caused him to behave in a cruel and inhuman way. He's not apologized or made right the injustice perpetrated on me.

Forgiveness is an empty gesture unless it entails correction. Without this it is essentially judgemental, rather than healing. In time we exist for and with each other. In timelessness we coexist with God. I am here only to be truly helpful. I am here to represent He who sent me. I do not have to worry about what to say or what to do, because He who sent me will direct me. I am content to be wherever He wishes knowing He goes there with me. I will be healed as I let Him teach me to heal.

T-2.V.A.15. (5):3-4, 17. (7):6, 18. (8):2-6

If I'm ecstatic with joy, it's through our soul connection. Every time I smile when I'm alone, it's through feeling his presence. His higher self has healed my inner child and indeed all my past, awakening me to the true scope of our soul transit that has nothing to do with the ego matrix.

My Twin Flame is a doctor who left me terribly injured as the medical complex maligned and tried to kill me for speaking out against corruption in their industry.

Arrogance is the denial of love, because love shares and arrogance withholds. As long as both appear desirable the concept of choice, which is not of God, will remain with you. While this is not true in eternity it is true in time, so that while time lasts in your mind there will be choices. Time itself is your choice. If you would remember eternity, you must look only on the eternal. If you allow yourself to become preoccupied with the temporal, you are living in time. As always, your choice is determined by what you value. Time and eternity cannot both be real, because they contradict each other. If you will accept only what is real, you begin to understand eternity and make it yours. T-10.V.14:1-9

As his cosmic mirror I was tasked with reflecting the truth of how he behaved in the ego matrix, and also the pristine brilliance of his universal self.

Let not the form of his mistakes keep you from him whose holiness is yours. Beyond his errors is his holiness and your salvation. A holy relationship, however newly born, must value holiness above all else. Yet reason sees a holy relationship for what it is; a common state of mind, where both give errors gladly to correction, that both may happily be healed as one. T-22.III.8:1.9:1, 7

Miracle working entails a full realization of the power of thought in order to avoid miscreation. The true resolution rests entirely on mastery through love. T-2.VII.2:2. T-2.VII.4:4

As I began writing poetry for my Twin the words flowed easily and included a message of forgiveness. Eternal love transcends the ego matrix and in my eyes forgiveness was instantaneous. So willing to lay down any allusion to less than complete love, I omitted the line about forgiveness and instead immortalized his abundance of spirit.

I ask nothing and forgive you all, became – I ask nothing yet you give me all…

Divine Love 💗 Twin Flames

You are the work of God, and His work is wholly loveable and wholly loving. This is how a man must think of himself in his heart, because this is what he is. T-1.III.2:3-4

My brother, you are part of God and part of me. I come to you from our father to offer you everything again. I will lead you to your true father, who hath need of you, as I have. Will you not answer the call of love with joy?
T-11.4:1, 3, 7- 8.

We are made whole in our desire to make whole. Let not time worry you, for all the fear that you and your brother experience is really past. Time has been readjusted to help us do, together, what your separate pasts would hinder. You have gone past fear for no two minds can join in the desire for love without love's joining them. T-18.III.7:4-7

There is no problem in any situation that faith will not solve. Only what you have not given can be lacking in any situation but remember this, the goal of holiness was set for your relationship, and not by you. Your faith must grow to meet the goal that has been set.

T-17.VII.2:1, T-17.VII.4:1-2, 4

Sharing intimate soul truth with a virtual stranger really made me step up to a new level of trust in the Holy Spirit and my own ability.

The goals reality will call this forth, for you will see that peace and faith will not come separately. Every situation in which you find yourself is but a means to meet the purpose set for your relationship. T-17.VII.4:5, T-17.VII.5:1

We have repeatedly emphasised the need to recognise fear and face it without disguise as a crucial step in the undoing of the ego. Consider how well the Holy Spirit's interpretation of the motives of others will serve you then. Having taught you to accept only loving thoughts in others and to regard everything else as an appeal for help, He has taught you that fear itself is an appeal for help. We have learned that fear and attack are inevitably associated. For fear is a call for love, in unconscious recognition of what has been denied. T-12.I.8:5-11, 13

The ark of peace is entered two by two, yet the beginning of another world goes with them. Each holy relationship must enter here, to learn its special function in the Holy Spirits plan, now that it shares its purpose. T-20.1IV.6:5-6

This holy relationship, lovely in its innocence, mighty in strength, and blazing with a light far brighter than the sun that lights the sky you see, is chosen of your Father as a means for His own Plan. Nothing entrusted to it can be misused and nothing given it will be used. This holy relationship has the power to heal all pain, regardless of its form. Only in your joint will does healing lie. T-22.VI.4:1-3-4, 6

My Twin was unaware that he denied his soul expression for the trappings of success in the satanic cabal. In his own mind he was a pillar of society, someone to be proud of. I was ashamed for him as I knew he was not created to mistreat his fellow man.

You are the strong one in this seeming conflict. And you need no defence. Everything that needs defence you do not want, for anything that needs defence will weaken you. T-22.V.1:10-12

God rests with you in quiet, undefended and wholly defending, for in this quiet state alone is strength and power. T-22.V.3:8

You and your brother are the same, as God Himself is One and not divided in His will. And you must have one purpose, since He gave the same to both of you. His will is brought together as you join in will; that you be made complete by offering completion to your brother. See not in him the sinfulness he sees, but give him

honour that you may esteem yourself and him.
T-25.II.11:1-4

I never blamed my Twin for his actions. He was blinded by his ego and I had to be a spotless mirror to show him the truth of his eternal self who would never harm his brothers and sisters in spirit.

In your relationship with your brother, where He has taken charge of everything at your request, He has set the course inward to the truth you share. Here you are joined in God, as much together as you are with Him. Here is the radiant truth, to which the Holy Spirit has committed your relationship. Your reality was God's creation. You are so firmly joined in truth that only God is there. He loves you both, equally and as one.
T-18.I.9:1, 5-7. T-18.I.10:2-3, 5

Let us join in Him in peace and gratitude, and accept His gift as our most holy and perfect reality, which we share in Him. Heaven is restored to the Sonship through your relationship. How lovely and how holy is your relationship, with truth shining upon it. Heaven beholds it, and rejoices that you have let it come to you. T-18.I.10:9, T-18.I.11:1, 4

You have been called, together with your brother, to the most holy function this world contains. The peace of God is given you with the glowing purpose in which you join with your brother. The Holy light that brought you and him together must extend, as you accepted it. T-18.I.13:1, 5-6

Once you accept His plan as the one function that you would fulfil, there will be nothing else the Holy Spirit will not arrange for you without your effort. He will go before you making straight your path, and leaving in your way no stones to trip on, and no obstacles to bar your way. Nothing you need will be denied you. T-20.IV.8:4-7

The power set in you in whom the Holy Spirits' goal has been established is so far beyond your conception of the infinite that you have no idea how great the strength that goes with you. Enter each situation with the faith you give your brother. Your faith will call others to share your purpose. T-17.7:1.9:1-2

Your way will be different, not in purpose but in means. A holy relationship is a means of saving time. One instant spent together with your brother restores the universe to both of you. You are prepared. T-18.VII.5:1-4

And when the memory of God has come to you in the holy place of forgiveness you will remember nothing else, and memory will be as useless as learning, for your only purpose will be creating. T-18.IX.14:1

Paula Rule

In that holy instant, you will see the smile of Heaven shining on both you and your brother. And you will shine upon him, in glad acknowledgement of the grace that has been given you. T-19.III.10:1-2

Reason now can lead you and your brother to the logical conclusion of your union. It must extend, as you extended when you and he joined. Here is the Golden circle where you recognise the Son of God. For what is born into a holy relationship can never end. T-22.in.4:5-6, 9-10

Every mistake you and your brother make, the other will gently have corrected. For in his sight your loveliness is his salvation, which he will protect from harm. And you will be your brother's strong protector from everything that seems to rise between you both. T-22.IV.5:1-3

And so you and your brother stand, here in this holy place, before the veil of sin that hangs between you and the face of Christ. Yet it is

Divine Love ♥ Twin Flames

almost over in your awareness and peace has reached you even here, before the veil. Think what will happen after. The love of Christ will light your face, and shine from it into a darkened world that needs the light. Think of the loveliness that you will see, who walk with Him! And think how beautiful will you and your brother look to the other! How happy you will be to be together, after such a long and lonely journey where you walked alone. T-22.IV.3:1-5, 6-7. T-22.IV.4:1-3

To all who share the Love of God the grace is given to the givers of what they have received. And so they learn that it is theirs forever. All barriers disappear before their coming, as every obstacle was finally surmounted that seemed to rise and block their way before. This veil you and your brother lift together opens the way to truth more than you. T-22.IV.6:1-4

Paula Rule

In light, you see it as your special function in the plan to save the Son of God from all attack, and let him understand that he is safe, as he has always been, and will remain in time and eternity alike. This is the function given you for your brother. Do this one thing, that everything be given you. T-25.VI.7:7-8, 10

As that was given you, so will its fulfilment be. God's guarantee will hold against all obstacles.
T-20.IV.8:9-10

Twin Flame Poetry

He is My Twin

I've seen him in the physical and I feel his energy

He communes with me in spirit.

He's appeared as a hologram before me

I've heard his voice whisper my name as the wings of sleep enfold me

He's visited me in my dreams.

His essence is my passion

His existence is the deepest revelation of me…he is my Twin.

Paula Rule 2017

My Twin Soul

Paul

Your Eternal Soul is my Soul's Twin

Through endless ages we yearned to be one again

Recognition of my beauty and power in the mirror of your eyes

Our first glance the most profound moment of my life

A perfect moment when you gently stroked my hand

A fulfilment of ecstasy I am only beginning to understand

Sacred wonder of pristine desire

A passion only Heaven can inspire

Our shared purpose is to exult in completion and perfect peace divine

To worship in the temple of love where there is no memory of time

For you are the magnet and I am the steel

Faint with longing I now have the courage to reveal

I ask nothing yet you give me all

Eternal Love is the Father's Call

In purity and innocence I love completely again

Thank you Lord for the gift of my Twin

Paula
From my mind, body and spirit memoir
God, Me and the Mango Tree by Paula Rule

Universal Self

Universal Self

You will awaken to your True self through spiritual ecstasy that transcends all else. This is quantum transformation of the highest order.

Only you can deprive yourself of anything. Do not oppose this realisation, for it is truly the beginning of the dawn of light. Remember also that the denial of this simple fact takes many forms, and these you must learn to recognise and to oppose steadfastly, without exception.

T-11.IV.4:1-3

What you believe you are determines your gifts, and if He created you by extending Himself as

you, you can only extend yourself as He did.
T-7.I.5:2

Choosing through the Holy Spirit will lead you to the Kingdom. You create by your true being, but what you are you must learn to remember.
T-6.V.5:1

The universal self is a revelation and evolution of soul. When I completely let go of who I thought I was; abused child, heartbroken widow - my multidimensional identity was revealed.

I am a golden ray twin flame earth angel. Golden rays illuminate through universal love. To nurture the seed of divinity in the heart of another is our sacred joy.

Those who would let illusions be lifted from their minds are this worlds saviours, walking the world with their Redeemer, and carrying His message of hope and freedom and release

Universal Self

from suffering to everyone who needs a miracle to save him. T-22.IV.6:5

Jesus demonstrated that we are eternal, spiritual light beings; here only for a brief time to help each other rise above the ego matrix to our home of universal love.

Therefore to heal is to unite with those who are like you, because perceiving this likeness is to recognise the Father. If your perfection is in Him and only Him, how can you know it without recognising Him? The recognition of God is the recognition of yourself. T-8.V.2:5-7

The energetic self is pure, peaceful, powerful and free.

Give as you have received. And demonstrate that you have risen far above any situation that could hold you back. T-17.VIII.6:6-7

You learn - that all real pleasure comes from doing God's will. T-1.VII.1:4

Child of God, you were created to create the good, the beautiful and the holy. T-1.VII.2:1

As you let go and let love lead you can see your old boundaries clearly and choose to release negative patterns your ego made to protect itself. The true self is a wondrous discovery of complete beauty created for ecstatic union.

Can you imagine what it means to have no cares, no worries, no anxieties, but merely to be perfectly calm and quiet all the time? Yet that is what time is for; to learn that and nothing more. Time is your friend, if you leave it for the Holy Spirit to use. Holiness lies not in time, but in Eternity. T-15.I.1:1-2 T-15.I.15:1

Your opening heart creates a new energy of higher vibration for powerful ascension. Spiritual light shines from your heart chakra, awakening other souls to remember their own celestial beauty.

Holy Child of God, when will you learn that only holiness can content you and give you peace? Call forth in everyone only the remembrance of God. T-15.III.9:1 T-15.III.12:1

Heart Chakra — Universal CPU

Heart Chakra – Universal CPU

Our heartbeat is designed to synchronize with Gaia and the Universe. Ancient peoples knew the heart chakra as the seat of intelligence. Jesus is depicted with a Sacred Heart, displaying the divine significance of the heart chakra. He came to demonstrate this truth so we may remember and engender universal principles.

When we feel love we are sending an electro-magnetic frequency that is received, creating a positive energetic connection. The heart chakra is our sacred way of communication and communion with our brothers and sisters. When we connect through the heart chakra –

different perceptions, locations or languages are no barrier – as no words are needed...

Could you but realise for a single instant the power of healing that the reflection of God, shining in you, can bring to all the world, you could not wait to make the mirror of your mind clean to receive the image of the holiness that heals the world.

T-14.IX.7:1

Ascension symptoms when heart and crown chakras activate include loss of ego, feeling pure love, angelic bliss shining from within and arms open to give and receive – in sacred service.

The quiet light in which the Holy Spirit dwells within you is merely perfect openness, in which nothing is hidden and therefore nothing is fearful. There is no darkness that the light of love will not dispel.

T-14.VI.2:1, 3

Heart Chakra – Universal CPU

Sometimes an energetic reset is necessary. As the Ancients built megaliths on energy centres to share the earth grid, so we attune our energy to receive power from the universe to strengthen our ability to heal, thrive and manifest.

Universal energy enlivens the spirit and activates the soul path. The physical body is seen as a vehicle to complete the tasks needed to ascend. When we live from the higher chakras we understand that lovemaking is sacred and only shared in love.

Purity and Sacred Sexuality

Purity and Sacred Sexuality

Sacred Sexuality is accessed only through the heart chakra and is the physical expression of divine love. The 'need' for sex is a sign of being locked into the lower chakras. As we raise our frequency and vibration we function more from the higher chakras. Times of celibacy are a powerful tool for energetic reset and elevation.

You set standards for yourself and the foundation is self-respect. Revel in self-care. Embrace your soul path with an open and trusting heart, and relax. These practices lead to self-mastery and empowerment.

The beauty of purity shining from you creates a cleansing and revita lising energy, within a sacred space of safety and truth that is healing for you and all you love.

Sacred sexuality is created by the universe, written in the stars, encoded in your DNA and accessed through the higher chakras to take you out of this world through a portal of ecstasy.

Transcendental Chakras

Transcendental Chakras

Accessing energetic fields outside the body is achieved through alignment to soul path, meditation, grounding in nature, working with crystals, and loving the self. Heal and strengthen your vibration so you can show up in the world with authentic power and beauty.

Earth Star Chakra

The Earth Star Chakra beneath the feet is your energetic connection to Mother Earth. Align your physical body by walking barefoot on grass or hugging a tree, swimming in the ocean or indeed any action that honours our planet. Communicate with nature by sending positive vibrations to the plants and creatures who share our Garden of Eden. The love of Gaia is ancient knowledge for ascension so feel the earth's resonance vibrating through your chakras to integrate optimal health and vitality. As we heal our earth we heal ourselves.

Soul Star Chakra

Your illumined self is accessed through an energetic field in the ether above the crown chakra. Activating this chakra consolidates your experiences in the ego matrix from your ancient, modern and timeless self. Personal identity is strengthened and expanded as you integrate the truth of your celestial heritage as a Star Soul in a universe of divine love.

Spiritually advanced souls are often depicted with a halo of white or golden light above their heads representing the significance of Soul Star activation.

Spirit Chakra

Connection to the realm of spirit highlights your spiritual gifts and abilities. There is no judgement or linear time here so you are free to embrace and refine your skills of Clairvoyance, Clairaudience, Clairsentience and Claircognizance. This magical kingdom is also home to your spirit animals and kindred spirits beyond time and space.

Universal Soul Chakra

Becoming a master of the world within and without through transmutation of lower energy fields. Adherence to universal law yields extraordinary power to co-create an eternal masterpiece of celestial love. This cosmic unified energy often heralds the awakening of the Twin Flame archetype. Transformation from I AM to We Are One.

Divine Stellar Gateway Chakra

Christ Consciousness is One with the Creator of All. Mastery of the ego self and perfect alignment with divine will is the power to manifest miracles of love and unity. This holy light being has overcome the karmic wheel for the ascension of all.

The 'Clairs'

The 'Clairs'

Clair as a prefix means clear. So the 'Clair's' are part of our operating system when we become clear channels for healing, transmutation, divination, revelation and more...

Inner vision is known as Clairvoyance - the ability to see through time and space through the power of the third eye.

Clairsentience understands by feeling the vibrations of others, plants, animals, Gaia and the Cosmos.

Clairaudience is the ability to discern truth and hear clear messages from the spiritual realm.

Clairtangency is downloading information through touching an object or person.

Clairsalience is the ability to discern a fragrance or scent from the astral planes.

Claircognizance is intuitive knowledge from beyond this consciousness. Just knowing....

We are awakening to recall ancient /new skills and abilities that are our birthright.

You have the right to all the universe, to perfect peace, complete deliverance from all effects of sin, and to the life eternal, joyous and complete in every way, as God appointed for His holy Son. This is the only justice Heaven knows, and all the Holy Spirit brings to earth. Your special function shows you nothing else but perfect justice can prevail for you. And you are safe from vengeance in all forms.
T-25.VIII.14:1-4

New Earth Community

New Earth Community

There is a light that this world cannot give. Yet you can give it, as it was given you. And as you give it, it shines forth to call you from the world and follow it. For this light attracts you as nothing in this world can do. And you will lay aside the world and find another. T-13.VI.11:1-5

It's the dawning of the Age of Aquarius, the Golden Age of love, miracles, joy and abundance. We are awakening to ancient knowledge of our sacred purpose. Our souls unite in the power of divine love to create communal spaces for spiritual expansion and ascension.

The real world was given you by God in loving exchange for the world you made and the world you see. Only take it from the hand of Christ and look upon it. Its reality will make everything else invisible, for beholding it is total perception. And as you look upon it you will remember that it was always so. Redeemed perception is easily translated into knowledge, for only perception is capable of error and perception has never been. The atonement is but the way back to what was never lost. T-12.VIII.8:1-6, 8

New earth comes through awareness of our unique soul path and the desire and courage to live its completion. As we share our skills and abilities we restore ourselves and each other.

All separation vanishes as holiness is shared. For holiness is power, and by sharing it gains strength. T-15.VI.3:1-2

Very truly I tell you, whoever believes in me will do the works I have been doing, and they will do even greater things than these, because I am going to the Father. John 14:12

The reflections you accept onto the mirror of your mind in time but bring eternity nearer or farther. But eternity itself is beyond all time. Reach out of time and touch it, with the help of its reflection in you. Reflect the peace of Heaven here, and bring this world to heaven. T-14.X.1:2-2-4, 6

Rainbow Rays

Rainbow Rays

A rainbow is somehow sacred to us, a miracle of hope and symbol of universal love and abundance.

From ancient times, rainbow colors have been associated with the physical chakras, and transcendental chakras linked with the properties of precious metals. These energy centers are overseen by an Archangel or Ascended Master you connect with through prayer. The presence of related crystals increases power and focus.

Awareness expands to encompass the psychic self where you may be drawn to a specific color indicating your energetic signature. Inner work purifies and enhances that frequency.

You may activate more than one Ray for your ascension. Over many lifetimes you may project the aura of one or several colors of the rainbow spectrum. At the end of the rainbow is a pot of gold, representing the Golden Ray of Christ Consciousness.

You glow with wisdom, shining your light with awakened brothers and sisters to co create a rainbow, harmonic vibrational bridge to the heart of the galaxy, initiating the commencement of new earth.

You have found your brother, and you will light each other's way. And from this light will the Great Rays extend back into darkness and forward unto God. T-18.III.8:6-7

The Last Judgement

The Last Judgement

The last judgement is generally thought of as a procedure undertaken by God. Actually it will be undertaken by my brothers with my help. It is a final healing rather than a meeting out of punishment. T-2.VIII.3:1-2

It simply means that everyone will finally come to understand what is worthy and what is not. The first step towards freedom involves sorting out of the true from the false. This is a process of separation in the constructive sense, and reflects the true meaning of the Apocalypse.

T-2.VIII.3:6 T-2.VIII.4:1-2

Paula Rule

Everyone will ultimately look upon his own creations and choose to preserve only what is good, just as God Himself looked upon what He had created and knew that it was good. T-2.VIII.4:3

Salvation is no more than a reminder this world is not your home. Its laws are not imposed on you; its values are not yours. T-25.VI.6:1-2

We are created to live in purity and spiritual ecstasy. When we connect to universal wisdom and communicate from the heart chakra we create miracles through Christ Consciousness and transform Gaia into the paradise it was always meant to be.

See the new effects of cause accepted now! With consequences here! They will surprise you with their loveliness. The ancient new ideas they bring will be the happy consequences of a Cause so ancient that it far exceeds the span of memory which your perception sees. T-28.I.7:7-9

Links

https://www.goldenraytwinflameearthangel.com/

https://www.youtube.com/playlist?list=
PLgZIUf1y6mMev21h-59-ZVvMUu3mzwW5_

https://www.facebook.com/
goldenraytwinflameearthangel/?ref=bookmarks

https://www.facebook.com/
groups/586736998391960

About the author

Paula is a Twin Flame, Golden Ray spiritual healer, teacher, writer, speaker, filmmaker, tarot reader, energetic transmuter and empath.

She is an earthangel new earth community founder for Christ Consciousness, Divine Love, Twin Flames, Universal Self, Transcendental Chakras, The 'Clairs' and Rainbow Rays.

Paula Rule shares her miraculous journey through her mind, body and spirit memoir – God, Me and the Mango Tree available in print and eBook now.

www.ingramcontent.com/pod-product-compliance
Lightning Source LLC
Chambersburg PA
CBHW040243010526
44107CB00065B/2851